# LOVE

LOVE IS THE MEETING PLACE
OF TWO ETERNITIES.

~*Francisco*

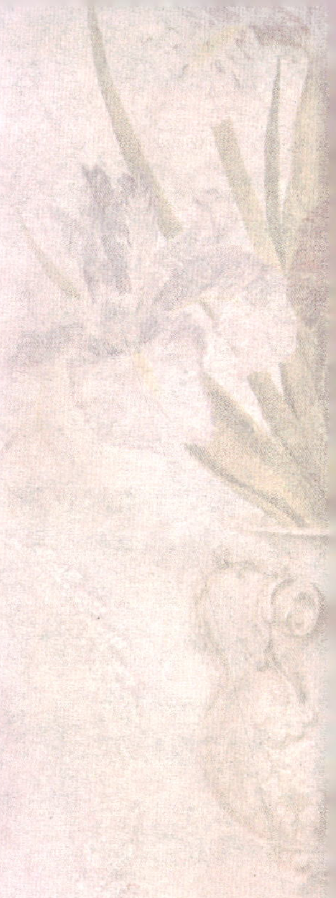

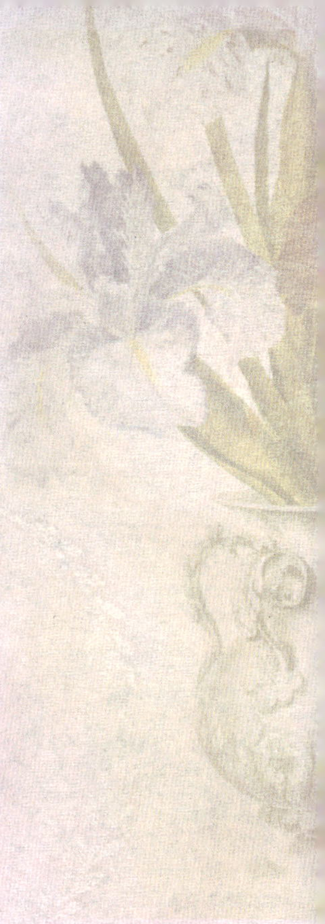

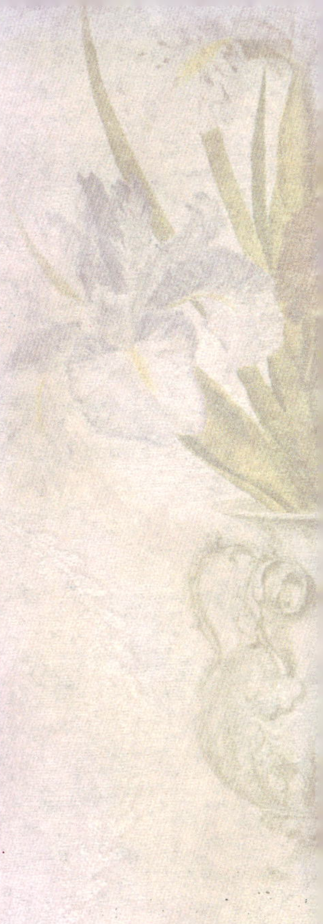

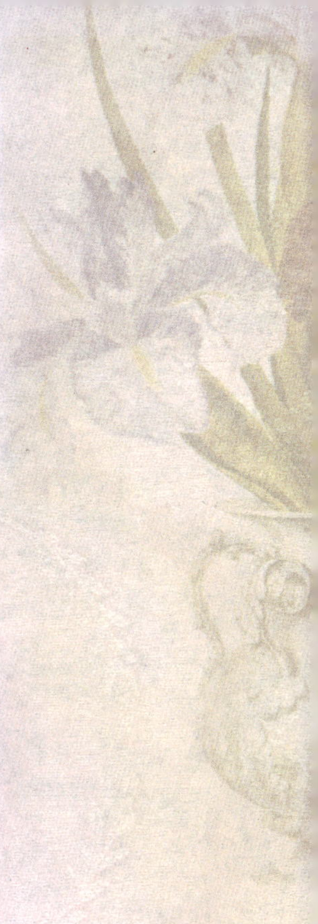

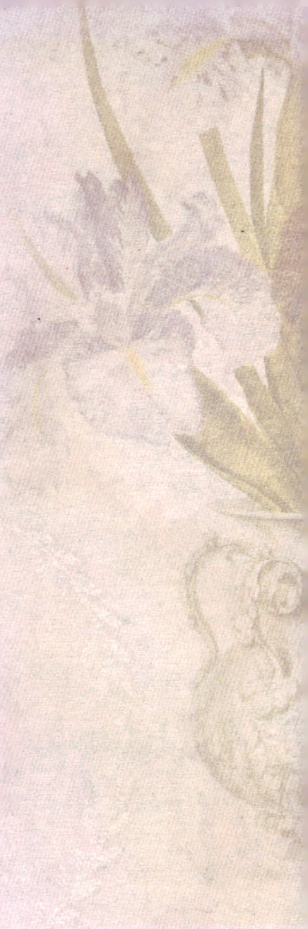

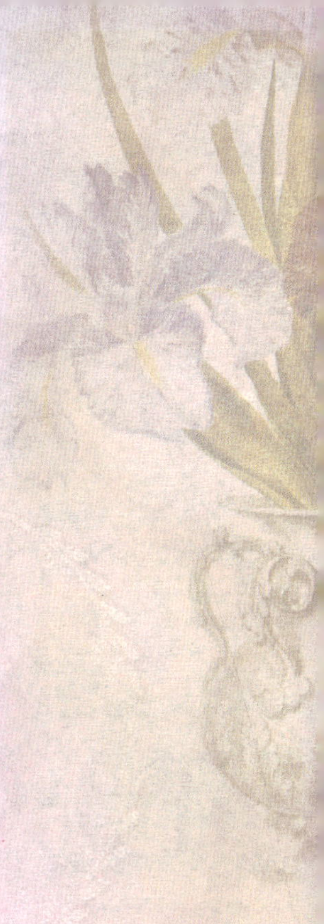